Black Wool Cape

Black Wool Cape

ALISON CARB SUSSMAN

Acknowledgments

Some of these poems appeared in my chapbook, *On the Edge*, published by Finishing Line Press in 2013. Grateful acknowledgment is made to the following journals and anthologies for their initial publication of poems, many of them under other titles and in other versions:

Re:AL Regarding Arts & Letters, 2017: "Anniversary."

Third Wednesday, Vol. X. No. 2: "My Joy":" "False Sister."

Miriam's Well: Poetry, Land Art, and Beyond, posted on September 28, 2016 by Miriam Sagan: "Baton Rouge, Louisiana, 2016."

Levure litteraire, 2015: "Alone Together:" "Letting Go."

The New York Times, June 9, 2014: "With Mother at the Zoo."

Lullwater Review, Vol. 24, No. 1, 2014: "The Joker:" "Foreclosure, Upstate New York, 2009."

Willows Wept Review, Summer 2011: "In 1942."

CCAR Journal: The Reform Jewish Quarterly, Fall 2010: "Border Kibbutz."

Maintenant3: A Journal of Contemporary Dada Writing & Art, March 2009: "DaDa-esque."

Cutthroat: A Journal of the Arts, Vol. 5, No. 1, Summer 2008: "Wrecks:" "Cape May Gold."

Hazmat Review, Spring 2007: "Zion Unblooming:" "A Girl."

Eclipse: A Literary Journal, Fall 2007: "At the Roman Colosseum."

Iconoclast, 2007: "Honorable Men."

The Neovictorian/Cochlea, Spring-Summer 2006: "The Fire," reprinted in *Meridian Anthology of Contemporary Poetry*, Vol. 5, 2007.

LifeSherpa Magazine, 2007: "In Montana."

Slipstream, 26, 2006: "Laundry Day."

rogue scholars.com, 2006: "The Night Rescue."

fulva flava, 2006: "Interrogation:" "Thirst."

decoylit.com, 2006: "Girl, 1966 A.D."

River Voices: The Poets of Stuyvesant Cove Park, NY: Kanter Press, 2006: "Marriage."

Confluence: Creative Writing by Authors with Disabilities, Ed. by Maggie Behle and A. Thorne Husted, Victoria, Canada: Trafford Publishing, 2003: "Solitaire."

California Quarterly, Vol. 29, No. 2, 2003: "Early Autumn."

enabledonline.com, January 2001: "Nights Up, No Sleep."

poetz.com, 1999: "Without Memory:" "Mother and Child."

Amelia, 1984: "My Father's Whistle."

Present Tense, Autumn 1981: "Dance with a Black Wool Cape."

Jewish Currents, January 1981: "A Moment:" May 1979: "An Israeli Soldier Dreams" reprinted in *Anthology of Magazine Verse & Yearbook of American Poetry*, Ed. by Alan F. Pater, CA: Monitor Book Co., 1980.

I wish to thank Rita Gabis for her editorial wizardry. I also want to thank Lisa Bellamy, Terry Blackhawk, Kim Farrar, Kathleen Kraft, Judy Michaels, and Diane Shakar for invaluable comments. And finally, to Philip Sussman, without whom there would be no book.

CONTENTS

"I lay there pondering my situation, lost in the desert and in danger, naked between sky and sand, withdrawn by too much silence from the poles of my life."

Antoine de Saint Exupéry

I

Zion Unblooming

Army children home from the West Bank, from Gaza,
with bandages on their heads.
The truck transporting them
churns soil to dust.

All around, the desert is unblooming.
Trees are becoming roots again
Then seeds, then nothing,
Sucked back down
Into the still ground.

There goes the irrigation system,
pipes have split, water has run out,
evaporated, into a dried pit.

The sky folds in, its edges pulled
Into a starless blank, a border beyond
All borders.

The truck passes
Solemn and dark.
In the back

2

Live bodies in uniform lie neatly stacked
eyeballs up, brains gone black.

Barbed wire curtains we have drawn,
around cities, villages, settlements,
everyone scatters to let the truck pass:
it races through, down open sunny roads,
then hits a landmine and explodes.

Dance with a Black Wool Cape

Last night I struggled with a black wool cape.

It gripped me
with sleeves of iron
and tried to smother my rasping breath.

Wildly it flapped,
a flag gone off color,
and cuffed my startled ears
until they begged for silence.

Then it rose, shimmering,
from my shoulders and floated
down narrow Jerusalem streets,
whacking on sealed doors.

But when I looked away
it returned in a flash and
flung itself over my body.

An Israeli Soldier Dreams

As I look in the mirror
an Arab stares back, frozen,

With glittering teeth,
black eyes,
and long thin arms.

He smiles slowly
but does not cock his head to the side
when I cock mine.

The moon slips
through the barrack window
and beams of light tiptoe through his hair.

He squats in the corner
with a frayed leather book
clasped in sinuous fingers.
As he reads
my head falls onto my chest,
and I creep off.

"There is an Arab in my mirror,"
I say to my commander.

He shrugs, and turns away from me.

Honorable Men

We want to get to know you to get inside you to taste feel smell your blood, we want to suck all the marrow out of your bones, slurp you up like so much soup, know the quiverings of your vagina, your screams when you come, we want to know the intricate clock of your brain, to take it apart piece by piece like disassembling a rifle, we want to put you in a box of all different sizes and shapes and shake it up and down and see which way you crawl, we want to put out the light in your eyes, we want to burn your tongue with our commandments, we want to tell you your dreams, we want to tell you it's important to die for your country and that if you die for it you'll be a hero, we've come to whisper in your ear to make you see double, to make you look in the mirror and see your flesh laid bare, to see the maggots eating you alive, we've come to warn you to stay on the right path, we've come to watch you in the still midday sun as you wander through the empty streets and you look up and see us pulling back a white curtain, we make you read to us in our language from the newspaper until your eyelids fall shut, we ask whether you write to your parents, and how many times do you write to them a week, a month, a year, we pry and pry, no detail is too small, we drive you into the shadows, we want you to obliterate yourself so you can come and live with us, oh yes, we have it mapped out, you will disappear under the sea like that diver, that English colonel who went to investigate that submarine in the Soviet Union, or we will make you play Russian roulette, your brain an empty chamber, the click ringing hollow in its deserted caverns, you shoot yourself again and again, but the dream goes on, you can't loosen it from you, you can't loosen us, we will stick to you like flypaper, like wet sand, like gum, like dogshit, you'll never get rid of the smell of us now and all your life, don't speak, think carefully about what you say. You might hurt someone.

Border Kibbutz

Giggling, whispering, we made our way to a turret.
Nothing there but the rough rocky nubs of cement ledge
under our entwined fingers
and fluttering spiky leaves of cedars from Lebanon.
Suddenly, floodlights flashed behind us--
a man in a booth lit up, shouted *"Atzor! Ma atem oseem po?"*
New volunteers, we didn't know Hebrew.
All we saw was the gun pointing at us;
we stayed motionless
Only minutes before Roger and I
scaled the fence around the kibbutz pool
to go skinny dipping, our limbs slick
we thrashed and snorted, kicked and tumbled over
and over one another
lost in the cool dark liquid.
And a half hour before that
we stood, pressed together,
in another American volunteer's cabin
while shots rang out
in the blackened fields.
What was that? Roger's eyes
widened like pools of water.

They stopped an infiltrator, someone whispered.
We were saved.
We laughed, unnerved.
A volunteer who had been there longer
than us said, you laugh now
but once you leave here you'll think a bag of cookies left
outside your dorm door is a bomb.
What did it matter that on the turret we were still naked?
That our clothes hung like torn banners from our hands?
That our bare feet stung from ejected shell casings?
Truth was, I didn't know which way to go,
so that when Roger shouted, American,
and the man lowered his gun and plunged us into night again
I thought, how do I get back?

The Night Rescue

They pull her out legs first from the collapsed building,
her high heels and ankles raw.
Her clothes are torn, covered
in splintered tile and glass.

A medic tells her *"Al tidagi,"* she will be all right---
He yells for a stretcher, she lies on her back, her eyes
stars that burn like fires from the bomb. Someone
brushes away glass, grips her limp hand.

She moves her head feebly from right to left,
as if she's reading some great text in the sky...

Laundry Day

She drags the bulging black bag to the dim basement.
The washers stand in a row, their bubble doors stare.
She unloads her wash—too short dresses, pants that don't fit any
longer, stained underwear from guilty nights spent behind
the garage—and throws it into a machine.
The clothes packed in, arms and legs askew.
She sprinkles a cupful of blue-and-white speckled detergent
among them, and pushes "colors" for warm water.
She cannot see the universe of the wash.
The clothes turn, sloshing, banging up against each other in the
primordial warmth, another kind of fiercely sucking womb.
A shirt is plastered to the glass, then torn away.
She stares at her bare legs full of mosquito punctures,
at the sweating backs of her hands.

The wash spins.

She thinks of a deserted street at dusk,
herself and other students spilling into it after curfew,
sharpshooters on the roofs of the shops.
Not a sound came from anywhere.

The soda bottles came in a dream,
like the basketball that crashed through a pane
of her parents' house.
Glass shards glinted in the sun near their feet;
flames flared, then died.
No shots were fired.

A Moment

I left you on the corner
Your dark curls disheveled
Your bones scorched in the sun
Your blue and white shirt tattered.

I raced through the streets
And all the while someone's voice
Whispered in my ear
"Keep your eyes straight ahead."

But my eyes
Rolled uselessly in the cavern of my face
Like dice on a battered craps table.

For a moment
I let my eyes link with yours
As you sat at the bar
Of a smoldering Tel Aviv café
And the smoke from our lips mingled
Then vanished in a rush
Of cold air.

No, my thin shoulders
Have never known your caresses
Nor have my restless hands felt
The ripple of your body in the morning.

Instead
My footsteps tread without echo
On the pavement.

I leave you on the corner
And fix my gaze on the road.
Every rest station is a booby trap
And my foot sticks to the gas pedal
Unable to retrieve itself.

II

Girl, 1966 A.D.

Somebody is crying in the back seat.
My little brother—I have his toy soldier.
Out the window a rooster weathervane turns feverishly.
We have come from Compo Beach, swimming until lightning
drives us away.
A leaf lands on my bare knee,
edges already yellow on this August day.
We're on the Old Post Road,
pass Catamount Road, where I thought
cats lived.

I listen to a talk in the museum
about a vanished civilization.
An archeologist cuts into a human bone
maybe thousands of years old. Does it still carry
the scent of blood?

To be a little girl on a rainy day.

Comic books spread out
on the rug. Coloring books half-colored.
Shoes off, raincoats on pegs in the hallway,

the rain stutters down.
In my heart memories rock. My mother
puts my little brother to sleep.
His white tee shirt smells of bath powder.

My friend pretended to nurse a baby. I didn't want
a baby.
Rain at the window, the world new as a nickel. Water,
the brutality of it,
the interrogator dunks his victim's head in a bucket.
There's a pecking order in families. Why
are we still so close to our animal selves?

Rain in Washington Square Park, on leaves, on benches,
on wire mesh,
on Washington's face, the world washed by rain.
I have lived a life that is no use
to anyone.

I climb out of the water in thunder and lightning, shivering,
my lips blue. My mother runs toward me
with a towel, then turns and runs to my brothers.

My Joy

raw spring air
by the sea, strings
of feathers round our
naked waists

o blessed were we green
hurling prayers at waves

then: "Miss Mary Mack Mack Mack
all dressed in black black black…"
our hair
like horse tails,

our wet bodies,
glistening, she went

my joy   this sister,
cancer took,
unlinked our arms
beach rose wreaths
our bodies

False Sister

One day Sandy said I walked like a duck.

I looked down at my feet.
"You do walk strangely," mother said.
I went to school in black
corrective shoes. Sandy pointed, laughed. "What now,
a brace?" My shoulder blades sank
under the weight of the chain
link fence in the playground. Sandy
stomped my newly straightened feet.
I tore her hair.
Did you know Sandy is an actress on Broadway? said mother.
I folded my arms.
During the class play, Sandy tripped me. I felt the scrape
of her boot buckle across my leg.
I told mother. She said, "Maybe you're imagining things.
You might be jealous of her."
I ran into my room.
I drew a pastel picture of me
with shiny high heels, and one of mother
with nose glasses and a wine bottle,
and the door ajar

because Sandy had just left laughing and yelling,
reeling like a drunk monkey with mother's pearls
swinging from her neck

A Girl

She was a stranger in her body, a dark hole at the center of her.
Boys always

wanted something. She was afraid she'd lie down with a boy
in the grass and give him

everything. Her best friend's brother pushed her
down on the bed, tossed her a dime.

She threw it back. He wanted to
pour himself inside her.

In the street boys used to stare at her breasts, never
at her face. She wasn't

beautiful.

Alone in the playground, she drew pictures
of food,

a drumstick, peas, and mashed potatoes, then
a table, a plate, a knife, and a fork.

She was making a home.

She craved a swimming pool and a string bikini.

Interrogation

There is this old leather chair that squeaks, it's black, it bears
scratch marks
and it has straps to strap me down
or I think it does and I sit on it

in the dark in the close little examining room and the eye doctor
twists the lamp so it shines in
my eyes and shadows of his arm and hand appear on the walls
and the eye chart

glows suspended in the dark and I read easily until the last two
lines, then squint and
make up letters, hoping he'll pass me. He doesn't.

He puts glassless glasses on me, then adds lenses. The lenses
get thicker, heavier.

I look at 3-D cards with swirls, dissolve
into them. He shines his penlight and I wonder if he can see
inside my brain.

Lights in the eyes, the whole world a shadow.

25

I am in a box. It's stifling. Water
will stop me from fainting, but he offers none.
I am taken apart, card by card, eyeglass by glass.
"What do you see now? How do things look when I try this?"
"Look here! Not over by the doorway!"
Irritated, just like my father.

I put my head inside the big silver machine
that measures ocular pressure and light razors
through my eyeball. I see the veins in my eyes,
little black blotches floating around.

The eye doctor badgers me,
"Is your mother still married to your father?" and
"Do you know you're one of the ugliest children
I've ever seen?"

Resist, resist, resist. It was war from the start.

"You're going to die," he said, "There's nothing you can do about
it."

My mother would say I was making up stories
when I told her what he said.

Under his hand, I grew into a monster, restrained
in that chair, in tightly fitting clothes.

Or maybe it is the eye doctor who sits in the chair.

Creaks and squeaks and questions.
When I am seven I have a Barbie who I undress
and I make her say in a high voice,
"Oh please don't hurt me," and then I have the Ken doll
step on her breasts, bite them.

I pretend I am a beautiful child, a genius, a spy,
being groomed by my doctor for a great mission.

Each week he gives me the eye drops.

As I leave his office, I cannot
see. Tears pour from my eyes. I cover them with my hand.

When I'm older, a new eye doctor says, "*That* drug?
You could have died during an operation."

I whisper through hospitals, waiting and examining rooms,
"I won't let anybody harm you."

Mother on the Beach

She changes from her clinging silk dress
into her sleek purple bikini.
She swings and sways down the boardwalk
in high-heeled sandals.
I carry her towel, wearing my torn sneakers
and billowing dress over my faded one piece.
I seat myself on the boardwalk railing,
under my floppy sun hat,
and watch her move across the crowded beach.
She drops her sumptuous red leather bag by the shore,
spreads out her towel, and spills back on it, belly to sky.
She smooths suntan lotion over her skin,
and settles in for a long bake in the sun.
My mother does not swim.
She goes to the edge of the water,
her hourglass shape blazing in the light.
From far off, I copy her, wading first,
getting my pale ankles wet.
Men's eyes follow her as she walks along the beach,
picking up shells, tracing their shapes with curious fingers,
then discarding them.

The Fire

Her father walks so fast she can't keep up with him---
His arms tight at his sides, his legs flash
through the street like knife blades.
His black raincoat floats after him
like a parachute. His fists swing. He doesn't speak to her.
He is a lawyer, gives orders to a secretary, scribbles on a pad.

Her father had a gold-plated cigarette lighter. Flick.
Did it have his initials embossed on it? It was smooth
and fit easily
into the palm of his hand. Flick, out comes the flame.
Click, it's gone.
So simple to make fire. She can't even light a match.

She knows him best from pictures. A picture of him slim
in his Naval officer's uniform,
Saluted by enlisted men. On a Colorado ski slope
with his second wife and their son.
His hair still dark, his face barely wrinkled.
A picture of him and his mother, the year before she died,
Sitting together, clasping hands.
Now his hair is white, his skin hangs loosely.

A faint smell of cologne.

In the street, anxious to have men's eyes on her yet afraid too.

She feels this,

like wet leaves sliding off her chest; the stars

at night, her father hammering on her heart,

flicking, disappearing.

With Mother at the Zoo

Years ago, after a long period of silence
I agreed to meet my mother at the Central Park Zoo,
in front of the snowy owl brought down injured
from the Arctic.
I don't remember what we talked about.
It was a gray, wistful day, a perpetual twilight;
the air smelled of snow.
We stood there staring at the owl turning his head,
above pale feathers and black speckled wings.
Many years had passed since we had seen one another,
taking those first tentative steps toward each other
in a kind of awkward tender dance.
The owl watched with his great yellow eyes.
Snow touched our noses
like a brush of wings
and we watched the ground turn white together.
The next year my mother moved away to California
to be with a new man.
When I heard of the snowy owl's death
I felt as if something had been removed

from inside me, some organ or other,
that the scene of our reunion
had been lost in the great shuffle of things.

Letting Go

When Arati told me she was moving back
to Nepal, she folded blouse after blouse,
her hands dark lotus blossoms, and said,
"People come in and out of your life,
some of them you care about deeply."
Shadows from tree leaves flitted
behind the curtains.
I stroked the clothing piled
on Arati's warm red velvet couch,
listened to the familiar slap of her slippers
against the floor. "Tea?" she asked.
We stood at the stove, her head just past the top,
watching the water boil in the gleaming white pot.
She brought me tea and rice pudding.
Her pixie face like my mother,
who moved away as did other relatives.
"In Nepal, my whole family is waiting for me.
You want to see the latest pictures?"
She spread her family out before me on the table.
I examined the photographs, and let them drop.
Some became moist.
Arati put her hand on mine.

"You must learn to let go of those you love."

The shadows retreated from the curtains.

When it was time to leave, I walked slowly to the door,

let it close softly behind me.

My Father's Whistle

The door opens
a shaft of light appears.

His fingers settle
like pollen
on my cheek.

He sits by my bed
building houses
from matches and paper clips.
Under his touch
they multiply into citadels
sprawling across his mahogany knees.
Under his hand
a platoon of cigarettes springs up
marching across the floor.

My father's whistle
fills the room.

I am a princess,
he is my prince.

From my bed I reign
over a fat pillow, a stuffed bear, a nightlight;
my head brushes the ceiling and stars.

Stepdaughter's Lament over her Stepmother's Sorrow

And she all maddened with grief
strews her body over father's
her lips glued to his like vines
and he goes down into dark leaves
with his few mumbled words
Death covers him, heavy earth gown
violets press up

She dreams of gauze, strands of sticky pearls
in the dark

And she cracked open in this hollow field
wandering through with her hair down
She bound with grosgrain ribbon
He peppered with fire
rotted rose and ash
gone is his smile

And she is dust

She is poppy seed and hayrick
worn to the nubs of her shoes

She is drowned in dew and mortar, pick
and shovel deep into the earth
She has become death

And the snow came falling
And you, Dad, hobbled on your cane
And she let me help you cross
And we were finally a family

III

Alone Together

Almost I touch you   One finger hovers over your hairless chest
Our lips come together   I snatch your shirt off the fire escape
Our thighs move against each other in the narrow stairwell
The lit cigarette trails smoke down deserted dungeons
of school
Making monstrous faces in the mirror in the boy's bathroom
Writing poems from a room full of drawings
Seeing the homework gods in their chariots thundering down
from heaven and anointing us with high math scores
Running from you in the playground,
The smell of peanut butter in your hapless tangled hair
A boy in baggy pants weeps in a small park and nobody comes
My watch broken, its parts shattered under the clock
in the subway station
We two skip over cracks in the pavement hilly with expectations
Caressing graffitied tree bark as flames flare up
The rank taste of fish from the East River
The salt taste of your tongue in my mouth
Brushing my fingertips across the jawbone of the sky

Explosion

I come to you, the water
sliding off me,
I step out of it---
We come together
like jade tree roots
and slick boulders
in the Arizona rain.

Mother and Child

Your hands skim
my face
moths in the dark.
The smell of camphor
on your lips,
your hair reaches
toward me,
the bristle of a silverback
slack light in your eyes.
In them I unearth
generations of houses
paintings that have been
swept aside,
porticos and couches.
Touch me
in this shadowy,
narrow room.
Let our feet mingle...
It would have cost me nothing
to be a mother,
my belly bearing fruit
to the world,

but with my bruised mind
it could have cost the child
her sanity, her life.

Cape May Gold

Dark fields, rippling leaves, 5:30 a.m.
A fish carcass cracks under my shoe. Bird songs burst
from behind my half-closed lids.
Mist surrounds shiny trunks, rain droplets shower down.
Branches brush my face, grass grips my ankles.
I trip on tussocks, slip in mud.
Colors blaze like gods on fire. Golden, indigo, emerald,
ivory, ink, scarlet, russet—
Motionless, a female yellow warbler listens
to a male's song.
I want you to love me again,
your boyish high-spirited body twisting
around me, while dawn shivers through the trees.

Marriage

March. Smashing surf.
Wind beats at our clothes like the fists of a child.
We plod toward the dunes as the sky darkens,
look for nesting plovers in the delicate brush sprung
from the sand.
We find pieces of driftwood, a shovel.
I recall my father's words,
"He won't give you a life of ease."
The gulls surround us, shriek when we take out
sandwiches my husband made.
Dune grass bends under the wind, swishing its skirts.
I wear sensible pants.
He walks ahead of me, scans the sky with binoculars.
The light shreds itself against a big Victorian home onshore.
Through my binoculars I see a sparrow battling the wind
before slipping into a bird box.
In the fog, we follow the strip of sand out
to the cement barriers;
we have miles of beach to follow beyond
the barriers, miles
of pebbled shore.

After the Party

On a cold rain slicked night
my husband holds my chilled hand.
He holds it though his fingers
cannot grip without aching;
he holds it as we cross the avenue
splashing through puddles;
he holds it as we hurry up Broadway
in wind gusts after a dinner party.
My husband's hand radiates warmth
into my numb fingers,
and reassurance
that he will always hold me,
even though I say, I want you
to outlive me
so you can find a happier wife,
one who doesn't stay inside
to avoid going out in daylight.
He says, no talk like this,
not allowed,
and even as he holds my hand
he doesn't speak of his pain
just raises our hands to ease it.

Anniversary

Touch me, don't touch me. Tentative,
my icy hand brushes your hot length.
You turn away, blankets over you,
impregnable. Moonlight crawls
through the bedroom window,
the cat's eyes blaze.

Talk to me, don't talk to me. You breathe
through the sleep mask, dive,
sliding through warm pillows.
In the living room you read P.D. James,
or play piano, blind fingered,
Tyner's free-wheeling jazz tunes tickling
the hairs in my ears.

Come to me, don't come to me.
Wok in the kitchen. Chicken in Teriyaki sauce
with broccoli and wild rice.
You on Facebook, appear at the table after
it cools. Each of us, staring glazed eyed at the TV:
Arctic penguins collide

with salesgirls in a 19th century shop.
Bumping into furniture in the dark. I open my arms
to receive you. I wait.

Nothing of you drifts down.
The tree near our building cut off
at the roots. My arms ache
from not enfolding you.
Black slits your eyes. My hands reach
for the fuzz of your hair
Once your kisses spun me
into the outer galaxy.

We are. We are. We are not.
Getting off the bus you go through the motions of helping me
down. But you don't touch.
Is it because I am a fragile instrument? Not more fragile
than your piano, moonlight streaming over its keys.
Uncertainly, you look at me.
My hand slips off your arm.
Slower you walk, I keep pace with you.

Kiss me, oh don't kiss me, I say.
And gently, you lean over.

Thirst

I was thirsty for you. I licked the brine off
my lips in the small room.
You were in bed, too sick to move,
the glistening tan of your arms exposed.
I watched you, rising
and falling.
Wind buffeted the little cabin,
I drew my knitted shawl more tightly
around my shoulders.
My bathing suit was full of seaweed.
I ran my parched tongue over my teeth. Everything
tasted of chalk.
I became bone, split
to the marrow, dried out.
I wanted to quench my thirst with your saliva, drink it in
through the straw of your sealed lips, but I could not.
Your lips too, were parched,
had little perforations in them that salt water makes.
The sun crashed through the windows, rushed out
through the door.
Starfish lay along the windowsills.
The pallid joint of a wave flexed and pointed,

gulls flew by screaming in hoarse, broken voices.

I arranged myself around you.

Your heart beat the color of dust in the narrow bed,

working up sand flies.

I settled my hand in your hair.

IV

Without Memory

I want to go to that place.
Water has no memory, neither does light.
Water over my hands, pure, fresh.
A day that burns clear.
I have blacked out much.
Memory is as deadly as mercury,
as poisonous as snakes, fire, smoke,
nuclear fission.
Memory can blow your eyes out
of your skull.
I want to be born anew at every instant.
Born from rain,
born like the cry from a blue jay,
born in floods of sunlight
washing over the buildings across the way.
Born from my bed, my nest, the egg
I hatch from every day.
Haul me born from my grave,
take me to where waters beat
clear and cool against the heartland
of the earth.
Bring me a freshet of fish.

Give me a name, so that I may
join the family of men and women.
Give me a country so that I may
die an honorable death.
Give me the gift of a blank mind
so I can absorb the world's music.
Give me me, in entirety, not paralyzed
or maimed.
It is the hour when light stands still
in the courtyard,
and figures stop hurrying to and fro,
and a long shadow falls from behind
a building,
and a melted watch hangs from a tree.
Memory. It will not get me.

Nights Up, No Sleep

CIA sharpshooters at windows
across the street. I shut
blinds, tell my husband, "We need
political asylum in Russia."

When he goes to work
I flee to my mother's apartment,
dodge American
agents, stay the night there
with my husband, whisper,
"they've bugged the place."
Instead of sleeping
with him, I lie with her, pressed
breast to breast.
A warped record spins inside my head,
"Clair de Lune."
I'm a girl again, afraid,
again, at night,
going into her bedroom.

Upstairs a radio blasts, in
my prisoner-of-war camp,

the CIA tries
to brainwash me.
I rise from the couch, hear the click
of a rifle outside.

My husband sleeps.

I sit in bed next to him,
cover my head
to interfere with the brainwashing:
towels, pillows, a stack table, to block electric lights.
This is how
they hypnotize you.

Lights flash from the club across the street.
There are two choices:
fight my way out and die
or commit suicide.
If I kill myself the gunners
might spare my family.

DaDa-esque

There are never enough pills to soothe the fevered brain It will happen so fast I

won't feel a thing My hand shot up so high Oh bliss, love again after all those

years of silence Branches strewn along the road, their tousled heads of leaves

dragging in the dirt The words on the page, DNA sequences Stroller

wheels rumbling over pavement while above babies sleep, dreaming of warm

milk Weeds grow over the road, grasses over broken glass At 5 it is still dark

and there is comfort in that dark Lose yourself in me The polar ice caps are

melting, falling into the sea After that came the shadow—blue, always

blue— I don't feel blessed The mad eyes stare in Old boots destined for the big trash

pile in the sky Anhedonia is the inability to feel pleasure It sounds like the name

of a pagan goddess My hands are black with soil I sink my teeth

into the raw sugar cane O that time would melt and I could rise

from the earth again

Over the White Line

Your brain's on fire, feathers fly everywhere,
your nest is filthy.

Last night at the museum
the paintings of Francis Bacon:
teeth and flayed carcasses.
A dog trapped in an electric grid.
In a picture by Leon Golub, a naked
man swings upside down while
two men in uniform beat him.

Outside the Cancer clinic, you find your car.
Malignant cells are multiplying faster.

Horror movies exorcise death: Giant lizards rip their way out
of characters' bodies, smash everything in their path.

It's just past twilight.
All the cars on the road have on their brights,
a stream of laser-eyed beetles.
You're lost in a wordless
fog, as the car shakes.

Image from a poem:
Twelve-year-old girl in Bosnia gang raped by soldiers.
They pulled out her hair
and kicked out her teeth.
You don't know which shocks you more,
the rape or the hair or the teeth.
You picture the girl: a gash of mouth.
No underwear.

You veer momentarily over
the white line.

You park in the garage. Let yourself in.
A movie you saw--mad doctor
made humans out of animals.

The house is still.

The Joker

We all saw it, the email, but nobody,
least of all me, his sister, took it
seriously, a cartoonish picture

of a decapitated rooster
after all, he sent goofy photos all
the time, we started labeling them junk

or deleting them. Crazy guy, he loved
kidding around, he couldn't resist

a knee slap at our family table
until he stopped showing up and hid
in Mexico, the way I withdrew

to paint in my studio. Now
the messages read "Please Look!" and "Urgent"
but we checked and they were still jokes:

a horse of brushes and my face on its rear
How much free time did he have? Wasn't
he sculpting? Dave went out to visit,

said our brother was nuts, living alone
near the border with a scraggy old cat
Who knew if he even took his bipolar

pills? His belly was huge
from take-out. No, not sculpting at all
When we visited him in the hospital

he waltzed with "Loony Luis" while we
stayed on the other side of the glass doors.
Still, I was afraid

I tried his cell phone dozens of times
sweating, fumbling around in the dark
but got his answering machine,

he wouldn't talk to me, he spoke mostly
with his hands. And the email messages
kept coming in like moths furiously

hitting a lightbulb. LOL!
The police found him slumped over
the terminal which had a shot

of Michelangelo's slaves coming
to life through the marble, a plate
of Enchiladas Suizas lay on the floor,

his gun stuck in the middle of the cheese.
Even in death, a last gag. How he did it
I cannot imagine.

Wrecks

Probably his mother once polished him
gleaming and bare but now
he lay in the doorway of the church, a big hulking
Goth of a man
in huge leather buckled boots, a ripped sheepskin
coat reeking of urine, calling out to passersby below and I
paused to look
at his bushy black hair and crazily crossed brows,
eyes spinning discs in their sockets, chest hair bursting
from under his coat.

My brother-in-law Benny—he was always the wild
one, the one his mother worried about most.
She showed us photographs
of a dark skinny teenaged boy running
into the ice-capped ocean.
Told us about knife fights with kids in school.
He slid

down a rope out a 5th floor window at night.
Five divorces and a tangle of kids. And painting, always painting.
My husband Mel, her other much younger

son, dressed himself, let himself in the house,
made his own dinner,
passed in and out of her vision and never quite
touched her,
in and out and over and up in a swing far away
while Benny climbed in front of her over the monkey bars.

Benny's face is a slash
of brown, his beard, an ooze
of gray, his eyes black water.
We sit in the visiting room with blue plastic chairs and tables,
all rectangular.
Patterns, Benny says, to make you go nuts by.
Sunlight slants through the ward, lingering in lonely pools
on the floors.
"Can you get me some cigarettes?" Benny says to my husband.
"No."
A man comes to take roll call.
"My name is cigarettes," Benny says.
"My name is matches," the man says.
I laugh.

Benny reminds me of a dusty broken old hunting rifle,
of a cracked wine goblet left out in the rain.

He took a bottle of Valium. It wasn't the first time.
His wife was at work. He wasn't painting.

I feel like an ice crystal, standing in Benny's aura.

"Can't you get me some cigarettes?" Benny asks my husband.
"I'll wash your car for a week."
"No."
Now Benny's eyes follow
Mel as he scratches his ear, adjusts his shirt.
Are they eyes of a hawk watching prey?

Solitaire

The taste of granite
in my mouth,
wash
of snow over
the palette of my tongue,

our bodies climbing along
each other in the night,

loneliness

I go down to the frozen
river,
gaze at its sleek imperturbable
face,
step out onto the bridge railing,
retreat.

At home
the cat with black fur
cannot console me,
nor can my husband

his smooth, naked flesh
cradled around
me in bed.

Tranquilizers do not mute
the brilliant crystal
of solitariness,

I step into that prismatic
world
and see myself from all
four sides,
the eyes

full of the dirt from fresh graves
ancient stones overturned
in the vapid air.

V

Baton Rouge, Louisiana, 2016

After Patrick Kavanagh

To Them he would always be brown, never golden
brown skin and eyes and teeth,
to Them he would never be summer,
forever winter,
his future, pore by anguished pore,
his hair, a thistle-wild burial pit,
to Them he was beneath soot,
less than rot,
hit for hampering the way,
a maturing shoot straightening stifled
in Their spray---

In Montana

In Memory of John Forbes

After a last hike you both take refuge
in grass--tufts of hair covering
dry, dusty earth.
You see the tall black tops of burned
trees, a dirt road that winds up
into the mountains. Red and purple flowers riot
in an alpine meadow. In the distance the Rocky Mountains,
and in the foreground weeds mix
with stalks. You smell fresh pine
and honey. Incendiary grass ripples
in the evening sun. Beams of light
pour through your fingers like ghosts.

Foreclosure, Upstate New York, 2009

Loose steps lead down to the dusty porch
surrounded by the graffitied stone wall.
The girl watches the sun rise from the lawn chair
paces from the small bungalow where they all live,
sharing cinnamon rolls, spaghetti, lemonade,
all of them stuffed in tight---
The blue coat of paint on the house worn
rough splintered wood underneath,
shutters squeak in the wind.
The roof leaks and her father curses, puts
back the split shingles and reseals them,
the sun high and hot over the flagstone path,
her grandmother grows tomatoes along that walk
near the boulder left sometime after the last ice age---
She imagines its ancient world when dinosaurs
and woolly mammoths roamed among the trees,
Now the lawn is crushed by dandelions,
red tailed hawks screech in wheezing elms
as her heart sinks with the sun on the planks,
and she slips into a place of buzzing voices,
her brothers plead
and her mother bangs the car keys on the table.

70

The driveway up front by the big willow
points away from the house onto the ruptured road
with millions of hairline cracks
fault lines to other houses, other families.

Hooray for Empty Lots!

Give me wild flowers, those sturdy thrusting intruders!
They tumble through the lot, creep the fence,

hang over the street.
The grasses surge up,

only to be stopped at the lot's exit. The flowers
claw their way through the chain link.

Wild and prickly,
what developer would dare venture in here without

a scythe, the weeds towering sunflower high,
and people's discards. Give me a pair

of baby booties. A Jimmy Choo shoe. A torn scarf.
A used dish rag, the pot over there, still with congealed

food in it, what these people ate,
what they used to cook their food on, the stove, all tangled

up in creepers, purple petals peeking from oven doors.
Give me Roman ruins,

the rubble of Manhattan
reinventing itself, a maniacal

shape shifter. Oh these flowers with their long leaves,
snagging the rain and sucking it up, snaring the soot,

funneling it down into their pistils, let's hear it
for the bulbous buttercups inhaling construction air,

buildings going up around them and they party.
Give me this jungle which allows me to breathe free

if only for the moment it takes me to pass it, but I return
again and again, letting leopard lilies brush my face.

The vines and flowers never die,
fires can rage through, but the wild flowers always come back.

Gramercy Park

To get there, I think of four approaches to a square,
travel back in time, ponder the little crooked swamp,
consider drainage, horse cart loads of earth, farmland,
and finally streets to 19th century carriage houses---
New York's first apartments,
then arrive at the park with its locked gate,
I prowl the shady streets around the green where people
walk their dogs;
hover near the oasis of soft lawn beds,
pass rows of trimmed bushes,
the pale pink roses, the purple phlox,
blooming so orderly behind the bars,
the neat ivy that curls over the gate
that keeps outsiders from trampling the park;
I eye the precise cement paths,
benches carefully placed,
the oak trees, their rustling leaves,
the mocking bird alighting on the fence,
It's nice, isn't it? The old manor houses,
to glory in their inviting atmosphere,
where no one in my family owned a key,
we were not of that circle who inherit or buy,

74

So here I stand, a supplicant---
I rest my head against the barrier, inhaling
the fragrant noon blossoms and the peace, entreating
the lady inside wearing whites to be merciful
and let me in.

M.C. Escher's Drawing

The hands are busy drawing themselves.
They come out of the paper
newly born.
Soon, they're greasy with the blood of slaughtered sheep.
Soon, they stink of gunpowder and liquor.
The hands keep on drawing.
They draw hundreds of tiny windows in a factory belching
smoke and fire.
They draw the door itself, a mammoth metallic thing, dented
and scarred.
They draw a woman in a shawl and a girl in a smock
hauling metal scraps.
They draw a man lugging a pail of water through a yard,
his cap sliding over his puckered face.
But always they come back to themselves,
smudged short thick fingers with broken nails,
flaccid surfaces with liver spots.
They draw their own shriveling.
Until one day they go limp and drop the charcoal
into the new hands under them, waiting.

Early Autumn

We're losing light earlier.
All that lost light, where does it go?
Up in the stratosphere?
Down into the crust of our earth?
Into our hearts?
How can the world
contain it, day after day?
Do ghosts of light walk the planet?
Billions of these spirits, trillions.
Dead light walking the grounds, lonely,
full of misgivings;
wanting to be touched,
held, wanting to be loved.

At the Roman Colosseum

The wind carries the breath
of the dead.

Sunlight brushes toppled stones. Yesterday,
I visited Hadrian's Villa,
his marble statues, tiled floors, and pool-with-a-view,
imagined Hadrian, slaughterer of Jews,
crowning his boy lover's head
with deep purple hyacinths.

Now, my floppy hat barely
shields me from the invincible
Roman sun.
I sit on a stone, spread
my madras skirt.

Would I have lived
in the Jewish ghetto
outside the palace?
In the house of a money changer?
By the sea with a trader of animal skins?

In sneakers I walk around fallen pillars,
cobblestone streets nearly
buried by grasses,
pipes of a sewage system—from 2 A.D.
People who thought they would reign
for centuries.

Am I a ruin?
My memory an artifact
in time?

I want the bones of those gone
to tell mine
how to live in this world.

In 1942

After Joanna Fuhrman

I hid from the Nazis inside a chocolate layer cake,
I tried on crutches, wigs, and white silk gowns.
Every cattle car
I slithered through with schnapps and sausages I blew
open with sticks of dynamite.
I was Robert Desnos writing
on the memorial wall for the deportees in Paris while my poodle
was being shaved for lice
I was Primo Levi drowning
in Goose Lake while turning loose red balloon photos
of Italian Fascist collaborators.

It was 1942 for a thousand years.

The iPhone showed me Auschwitz on Google.
Google showed me the train tracks.
It was 1942 when I received potatoes from outside
the Warsaw Ghetto.
It was 1942

when Eli Wiesel saved
the Jewish cemetery in Sighet by shielding the headstones
with hundreds of white doves.

I was Anne Frank's age
I was not Anne Frank's age.

I ate every Jewish star
ripping them off people's coats.

I collected cyanide pills "just in case"
and downloaded *I Will Survive* by Sala Pawlowicz.
I rode a bucking bronco into Polish gestapo headquarters.
It was the Russian winter
of lassoing Nazi dive bombers in the snow,
the panzers got stuck in piles of Rembrandts.
I was excited by the idea of disguising myself

more than the escape---
I parachuted out of a plane on a secret mission
carrying fifty five frogs.
I smuggled whipped cream pies packed with bullets
to the Resistance
and wrote the words "Nazis *Raus*!"
on top of my fellow fighter's roof.

I covered every inch of my house with swelling wedding veils.
I had eleven children,
and everyone in the world
heard the music of their laughter.

Notes

The poem, "Border Kibbutz," is inspired by Major Jackson's poem, "Selling Out," which appeared in his book of poetry *Hoops*, published by W.W. Norton in New York, NY, 2006.

In the poem "My Joy," the lines "Miss Mary Mack Mack Mack…" are taken from "Miss Mary Mack," a game of clapping played by children in English-speaking nations.

The poem "Without Memory" uses images drawn from the paintings *Mystery and Melancholy of a Street*, by Giorgio de Chirico and *The Persistence of Memory* by Salvador Dali.

In "Over the White Line" reference is made to a poem about rape and murder in the Balkans called "Terminus" by Nicholas Christopher which was posted in *Salon* on March 9, 2000 at 10:00 pm.

The poem "Baton Rouge, Louisiana, 2016" refers to July 5, 2016, when, as stated in *Time* magazine,"Police in Baton Rouge [LA] fatally shot Alton Sterling, a 37-year-old black man, in an encounter that was largely captured on video and raised widespread concerns about the officers' actions."

"In 1942" makes reference to the following:

83

Robert Desnos: a French surrealist poet and "an influential part of the burgeoning surrealist movement. Friendship with the group [in the 1920s] helped Desnos develop his writing practice, and he drew extensively on the automatic writing techniques for which surrealism became famous," according to *Poetry* magazine.

Primo Levi: As stated by *The Atlantic*, Levi was best known for his Holocaust memoir *If This is a Man* [*Survival in Auschwitz*], as well as for *The Periodic Table*---a book about his life, in, with, and through, chemistry...". He died in 1987.

Elie Wiesel: Wiesel was a survivor of Auschwitz, a Nobel Peace Prize winner, and the author of the Holocaust memoir *Night*, among many other books. As stated by *The New York Times*, "he became an eloquent witness to the memory of the six million Jews slaughtered during World War II." He died in 2016.

Anne Frank: According to *Britannica*, Frank was "a Jewish girl whose diary of her family's two years in hiding during the German occupation of the Netherlands became a classic of war literature."

Jewish stars: As stated by the *British Library, Learning: Voices of the Holocaust*, "Jews throughout Nazi-occupied Europe were forced to wear a badge in the form of a yellow star as a means of identification.

About the Author

Alison Carb Sussman, a 2015 Pushcart Prize nominee, has garnered numerous awards and publications throughout her writing career. Her chapbook, *On the Edge*, was published by Finishing Line Press in 2013. Sussman won the Abroad Writers' Conference/Finishing Line Press Authors Poetry Contest and read her winning poems as their guest in Dublin, Ireland in 2015. Her poem "Dirty" was a finalist in *Naugatuck River Review's* 11th Annual Narrative Poetry Contest in 2019. Her poem "Anhedonia" (now "Anhedonic Woman") was a finalist in the 49th Parallel Award for Poetry in *Bellingham Review's* 2016 Literary Contests. Her poems have appeared in *Atlanta Review, Cutthroat: A Journal of the Arts, Gargoyle, The New York Times, Rattle, Southword,* and other publications. She lives and writes in New York City.

About the Press

Unsolicited Press was founded in 2012 and is based in Portland, Oregon. The small press publishes fiction, poetry, and creative nonfiction written by award-winning and emerging authors. Some of its authors include John W. Bateman, Anne Leigh Parrish, Adrian Ernesto Cepeda, and Raki Kopernik.

Learn more at www.unsolicitedpress.com

formation can be obtained
CGtesting.com
the USA
0005140822
BV00002B/135

9 781950 730896